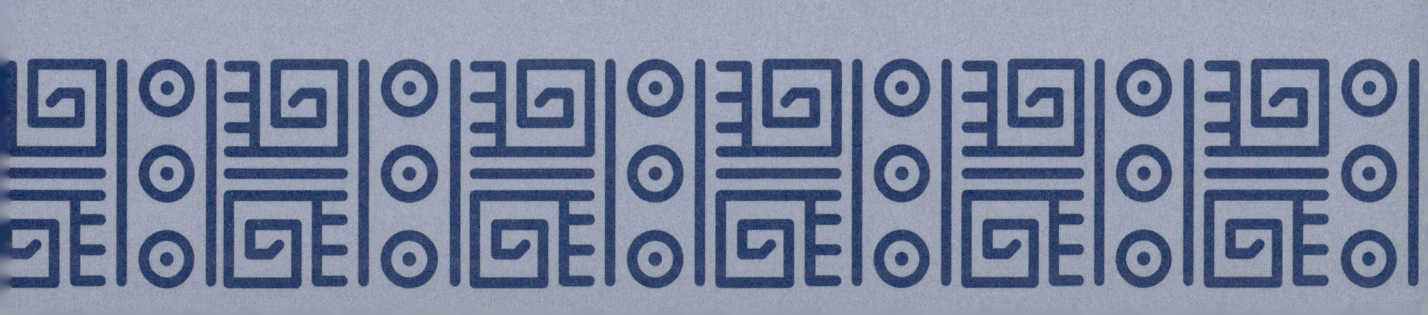

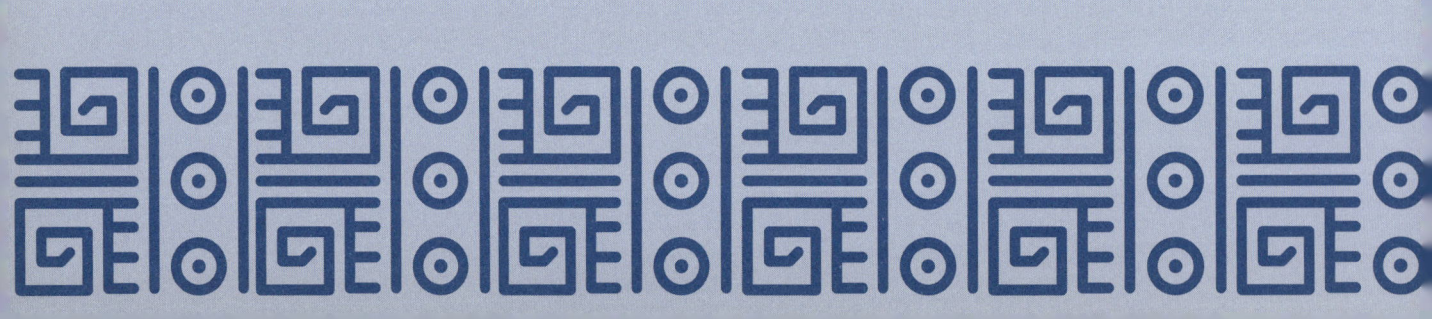

JESUS AND THE NEPHITES

For Darcy

© 2021 Deseret Book Company

Illustrations © 2021 Kevin Keele

All rights reserved. No part of this book may be reproduced in any form or by any means without permission in writing from the publisher, Deseret Book Company, at permissions@deseretbook.com or P. O. Box 30178, Salt Lake City, Utah 84130. This work is not an official publication of The Church of Jesus Christ of Latter-day Saints. The views expressed herein are the responsibility of the author and do not necessarily represent the position of the Church or of Deseret Book Company.

Deseret Book is a registered trademark of Deseret Book Company.

Visit us at DeseretBook.com

Library of Congress Cataloging-in-Publication Data
(CIP on file)
ISBN 978-1-62972-879-7

Printed in China
RR Donnelley, Dongguan, China

10/2020

10 9 8 7 6 5 4 3 2 1

JESUS AND THE NEPHITES

THE FIRST EASTER IN THE NEW WORLD

Illustrated by Kevin Keele

DESERET BOOK

Salt Lake City, Utah

Like the people in Jerusalem, the people in the Americas were taught many things about Jesus Christ.
(1 Nephi 11:27–29)

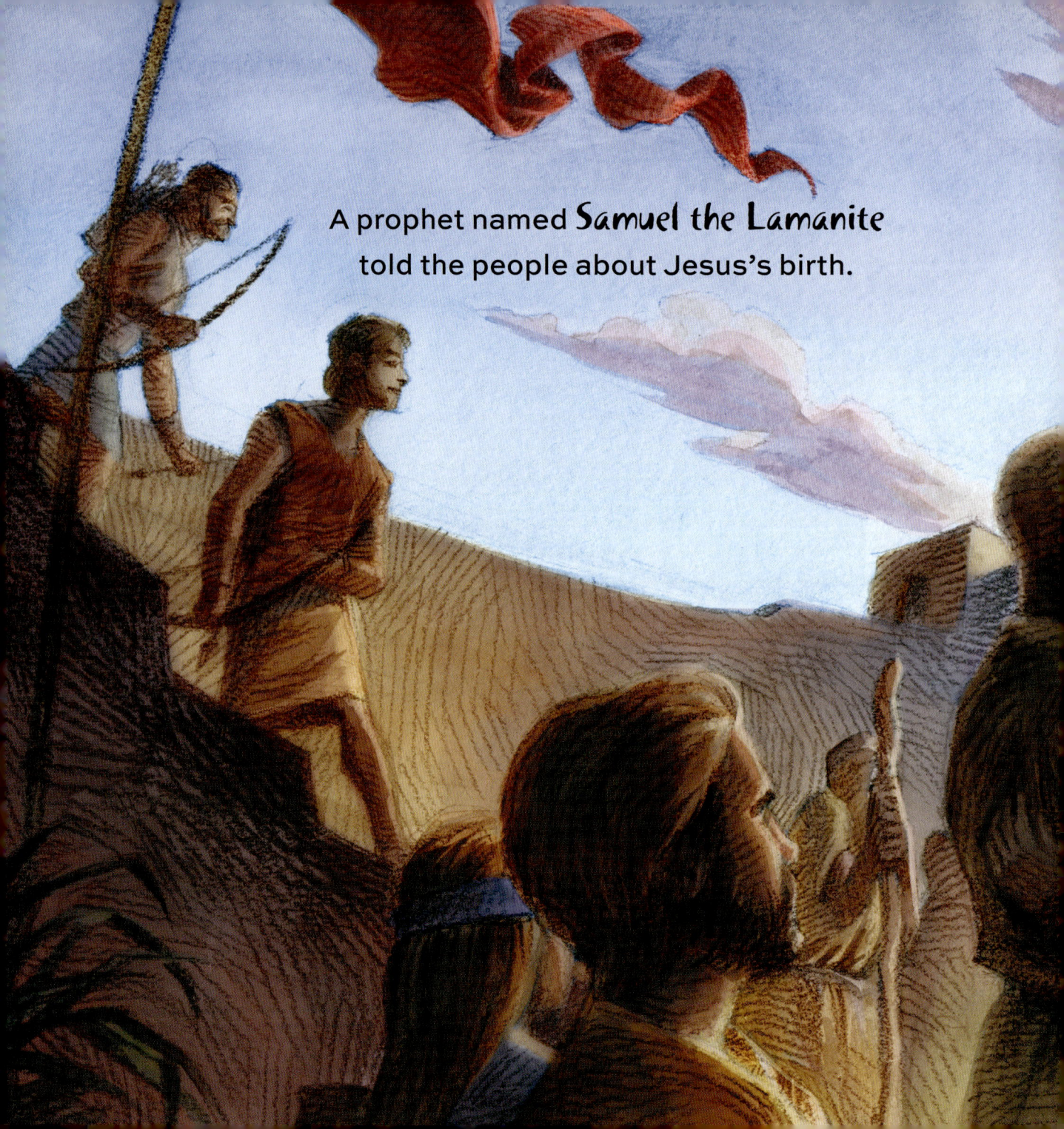

A prophet named **Samuel the Lamanite** told the people about Jesus's birth.

Samuel also told them what signs they would see when Jesus was crucified.
(Helaman 14:1–7, 20–28)

When the storms and earthquakes and fires stopped, *darkness filled the land.* The darkness was so thick that no light could be seen, not even from the moon or the stars.

(3 Nephi 8:19–22)

He healed the people who were sick, deaf, and blind. The people were so grateful, they bowed down and kissed His feet, and their tears fell on His feet.
(3 Nephi 17:6–10)

Then Jesus *gathered the little children* and blessed each one. The heavens opened, and angels came down and ministered to the children.
(3 Nephi 17:11–12, 21–24)

But Jesus could not stay with the Nephites forever. He ascended back into heaven, and the Nephites rejoiced that Jesus had visited them.

Every Easter, and all year, we can rejoice like the Nephites did. We can be baptized and remember Jesus each time we take the sacrament, and we can try to be more like Him every day.
(3 Nephi 27:20–22)

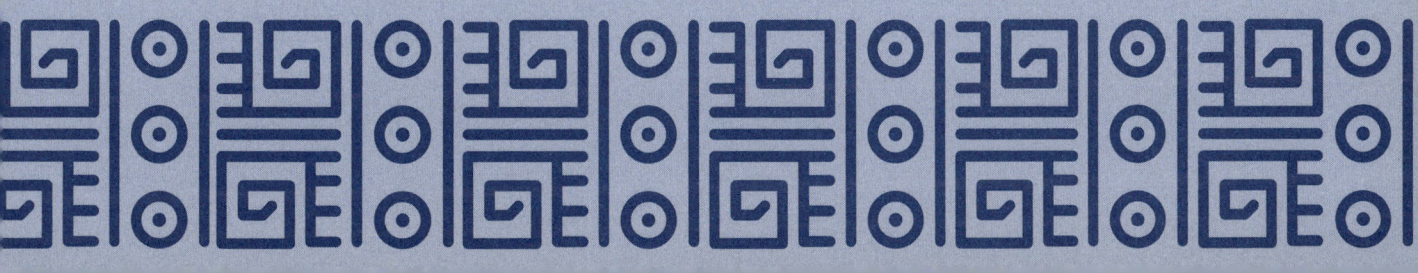